The aMAZEing journey of... MARCO POLO

ANNA NILSEN

To Fi
– From ATB

Published by Little Hare Books
45 Cooper Street, Surry Hills
NSW 2010 AUSTRALIA

Copyright © Anna Nilsen 2002

First published in 2002

National Library of Australia
Cataloguing-in-Publication entry

Nilsen, Anna.
    The amazeing journey of Marco Polo.

    For children.
    ISBN 1 877003 12 3.

    1. Maze puzzles - Juvenile literature. I. Title.

793.738

Designed by Louise McGeachie
Printed in Hong Kong
Produced by Phoenix Offset

5 4 3 2 1

Take the journey of a lifetime!

Follow in the footsteps of the explorer Marco Polo in this amazing real-life maze adventure. In 1271, when Marco was only 17, he travelled with his father and uncle from their home in Venice, Italy to the palace of the great emperor Kublai Khan in Khanabalik (now called Beijing), China.

Beware—this is a perilous voyage. You must sail through seas filled with terrifying monsters, climb the world's highest mountains and cross the treacherous Takla Makan Desert.

Start each maze at the green flag on the left-hand page and find your way to the red flag on the right. Then, when you have completed the mazes, there are 12 extra tasks at the back of the book.

Good luck—and safe journey!

The journey of Marco Polo

 Venice

 The Mediterranean

 Jerusalem

 Ezerum

 Roof of the World

 Kashmir

 Takla Makan Desert

 Dunhuang Caves

 Kanchow

 Ningxia

 Shangtu

 Khanabalik

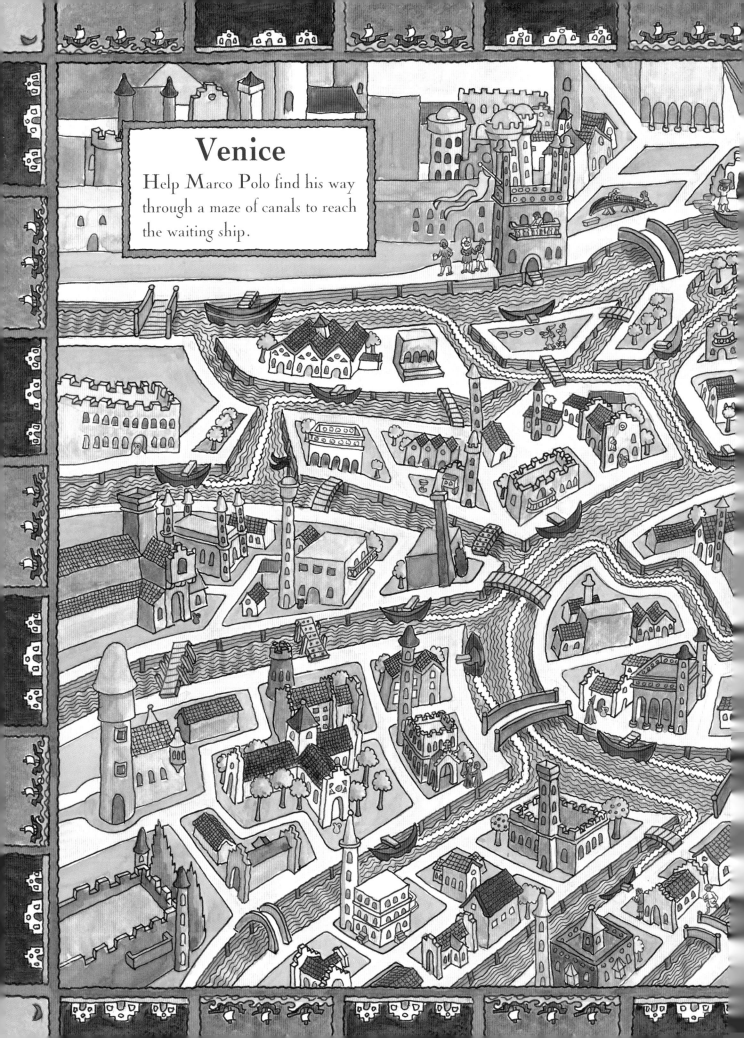

Venice

Help Marco Polo find his way through a maze of canals to reach the waiting ship.

The Mediterranean

Whiz along the backs of the sea serpents, but there's a catch: you can only travel from tail to head. Watch out for whirlpools—and hungry monsters!

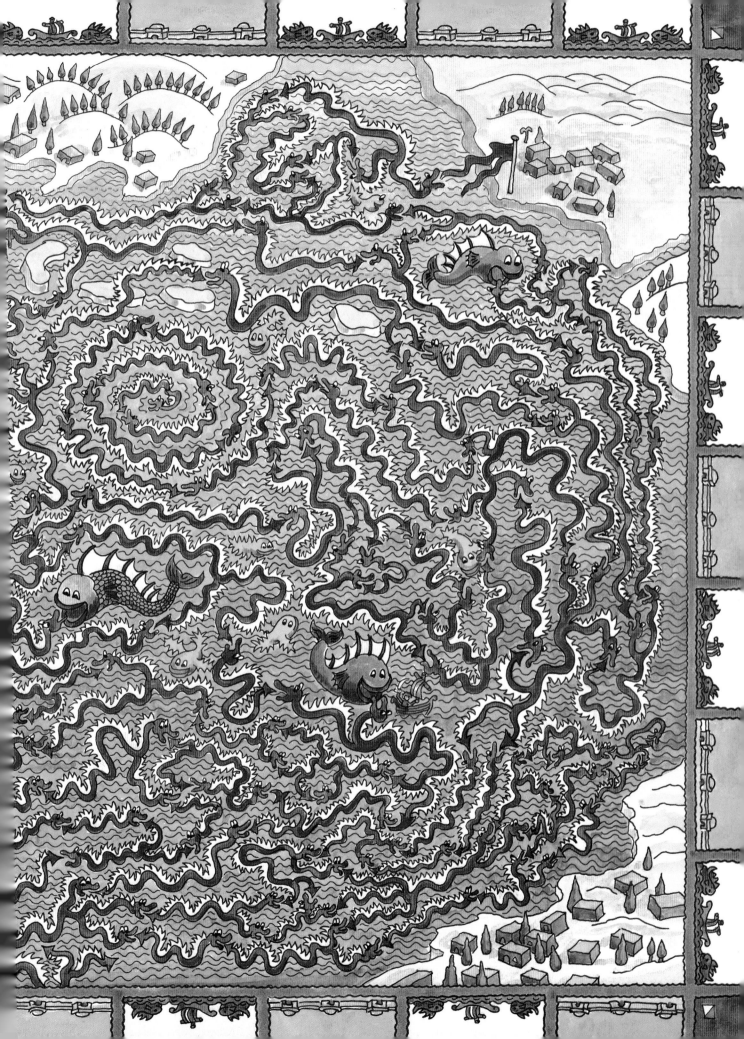

Jerusalem

Take care—you could easily get lost in the winding streets of this holy city!

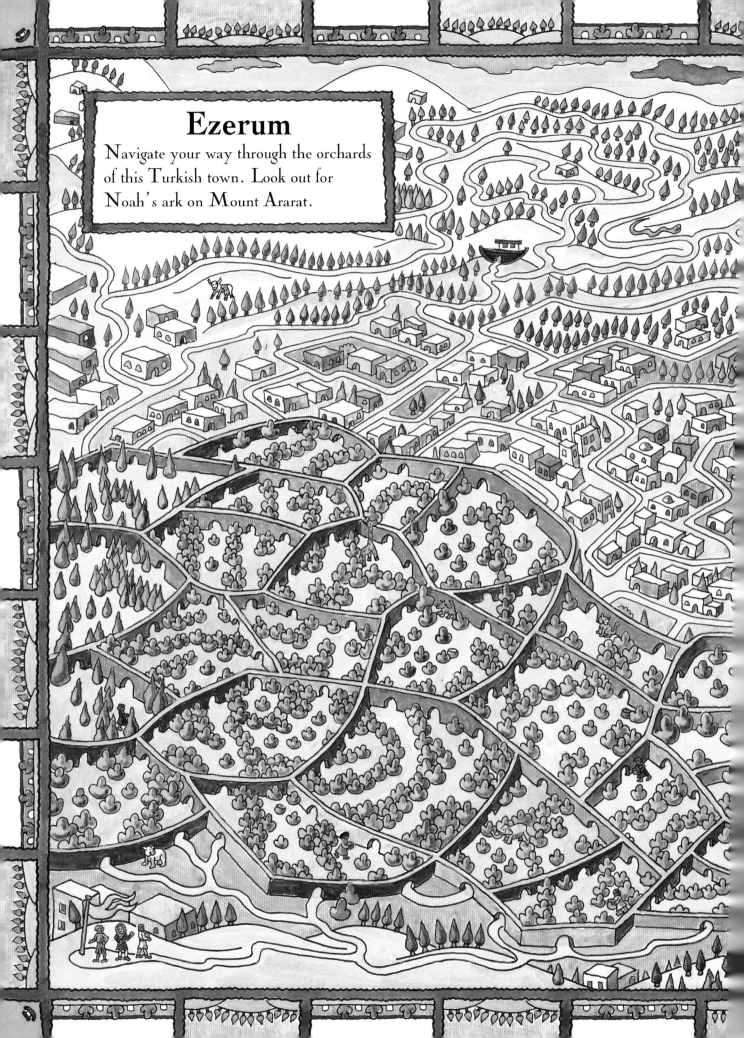

Ezerum

Navigate your way through the orchards of this Turkish town. Look out for Noah's ark on Mount Ararat.

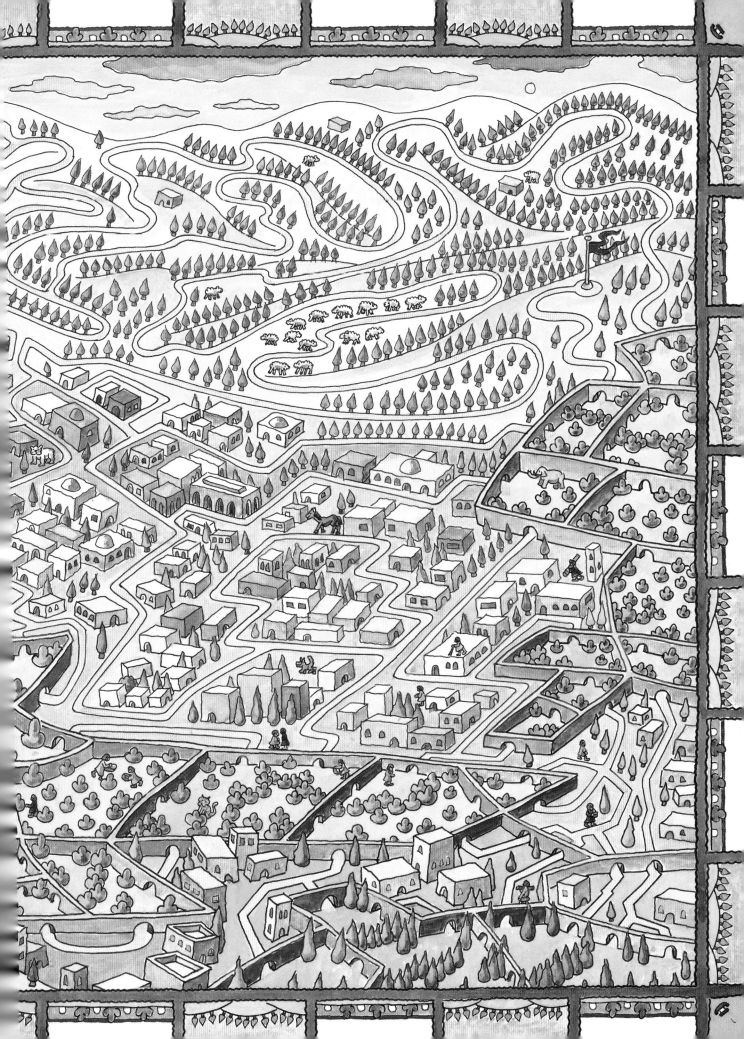

Roof of the World

Pass through the arches and wind your way up and down this rough mountain pass. Take deep breaths—the air is very thin up here!

Kashmir

Glide across beautiful lakes and slide
down snowy slopes on your way to
the highest peak.

Takla Makan Desert

Trace your path slowly and carefully through the singing sands—many travellers haven't survived…

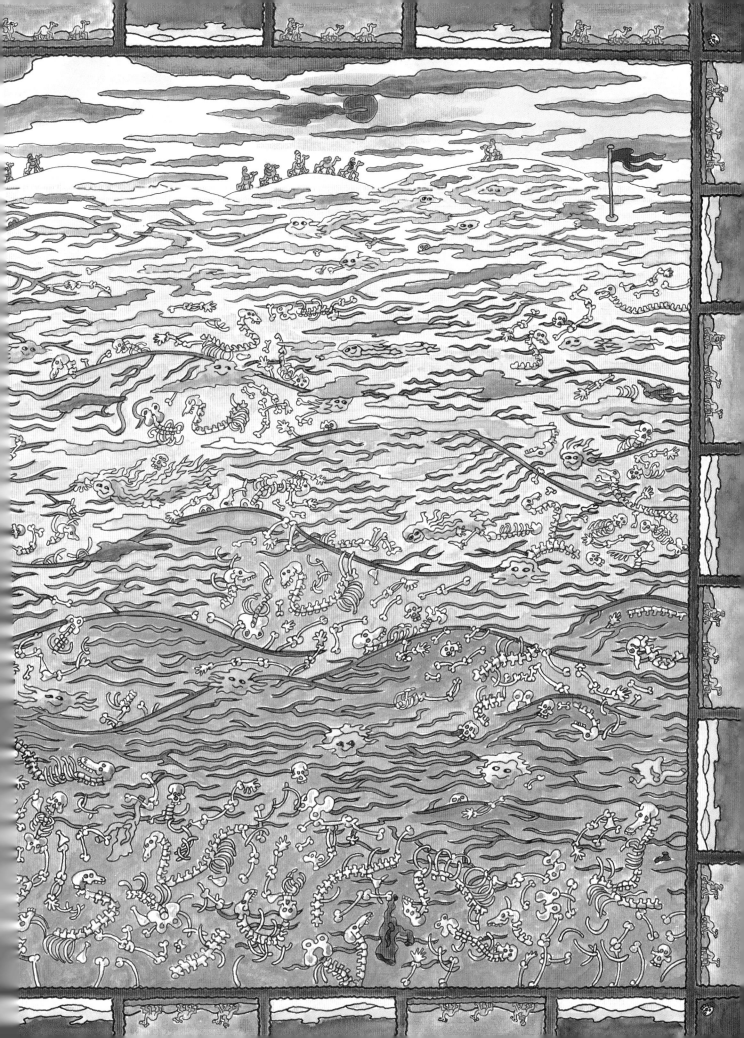

Dunhuang Caves

Follow the lanterns through the dead of night. Once past the caves, you must climb the craggy cliffs.

Kanchow

Buy some silk at this busy trading station
—you could even haggle for a camel before
heading off into the Gobi Desert.

Ningxia

The beautiful bridges, lakes and pagodas of these Chinese gardens are very restful—except if you can't find your way out again!

Shangtu

Join the Great Khan's hunting party—but try to avoid being trampled by the horses' hooves!

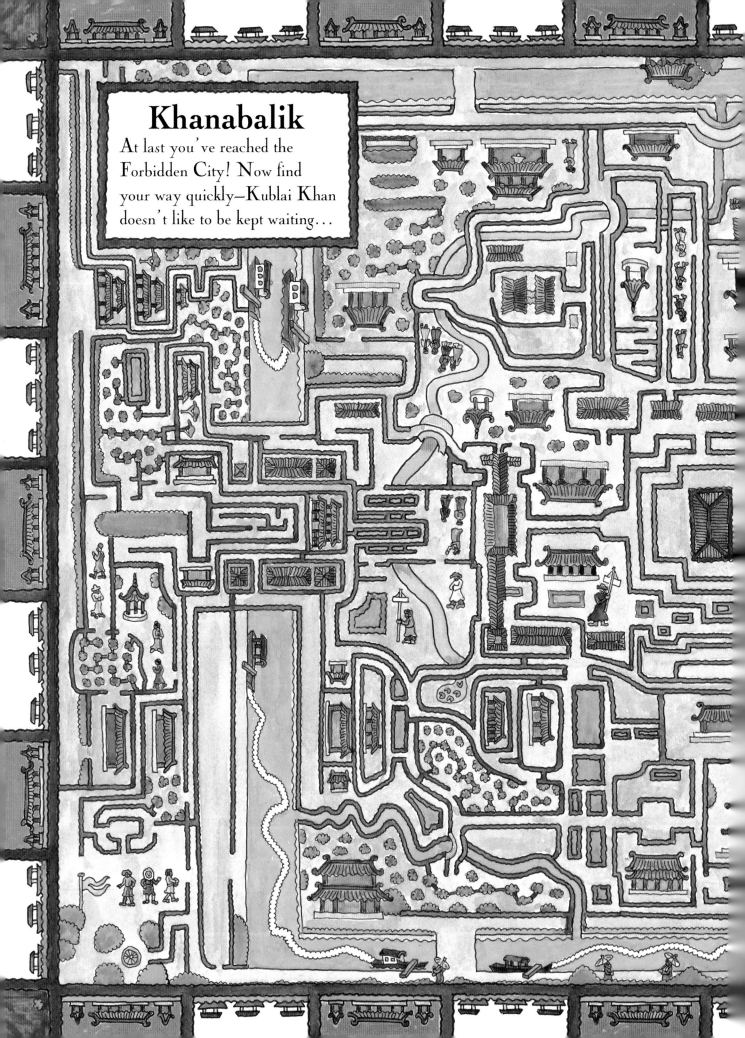

Khanabalik

At last you've reached the Forbidden City! Now find your way quickly—Kublai Khan doesn't like to be kept waiting…

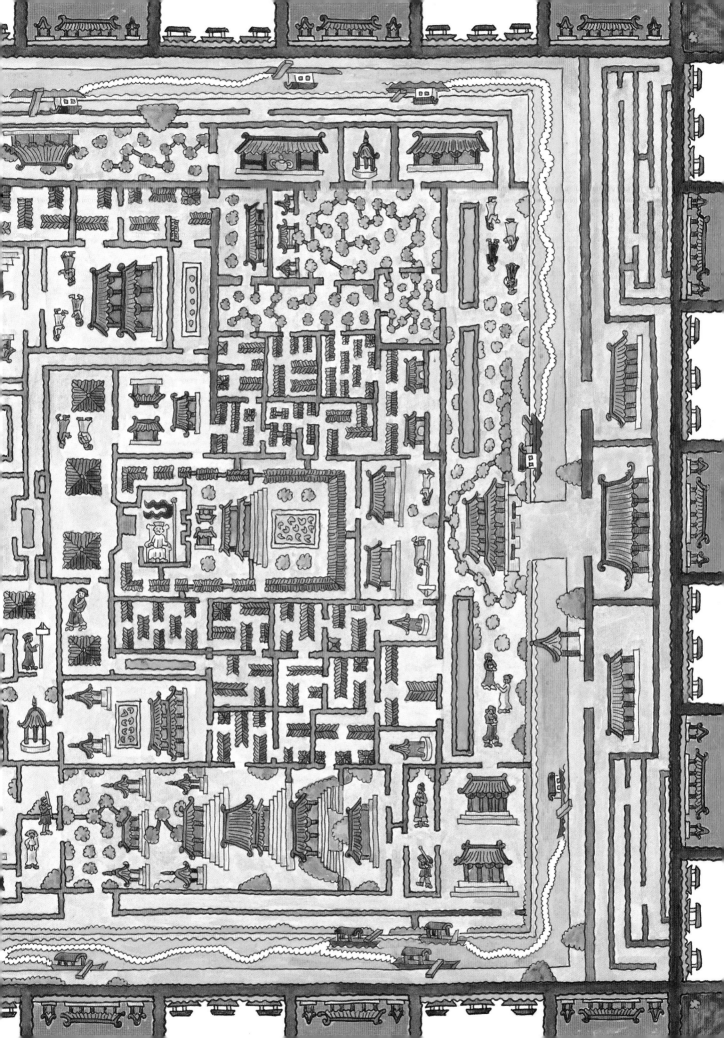

Puzzles

For an extra challenge, try to solve these puzzles.

Venice

How many gold water jugs can you find?

The Mediterranean

How many pirates with gold sabres are
waiting to pounce?

Jerusalem

Help Marco collect the pot of oil from Herod's
temple to take to Kublai Khan.

Ezerum

How many pairs of animals can you find?

Roof of the World

Help Marco reach the yurt being drawn
by cattle.

Kashmir

Can you find the way to the floating garden
in the lake?

Takla Makan Desert
Find the ghostly camel.

Dunhuang Caves
How many priests carrying candles can you find?

Kanchow
Look for a camel with two humps.

Ningxia
How many dragon statues with wings can you find?
Now find one without wings!

Shangtu
Can you find the wild boar?

Khanabalik
Find the oil, and help Marco deliver
it to Kublai Khan.

Solutions!

These are the most direct routes through the mazes.

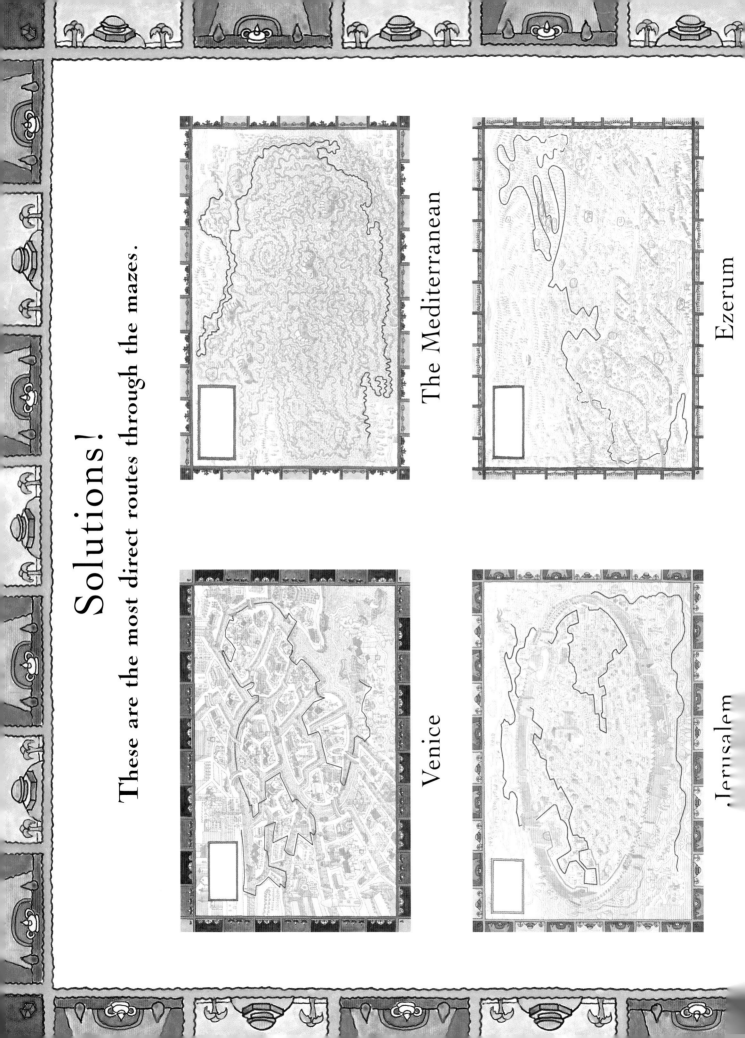

The Mediterranean

Ezerum

Venice

Jerusalem

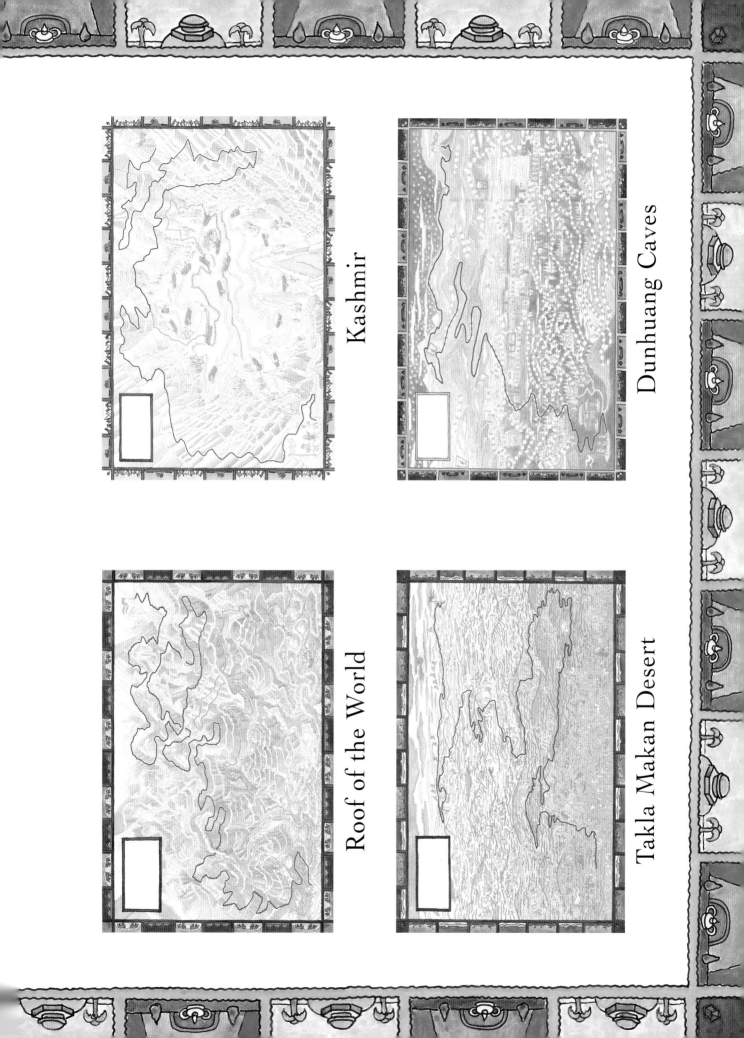

Kashmir

Dunhuang Caves

Roof of the World

Takla Makan Desert

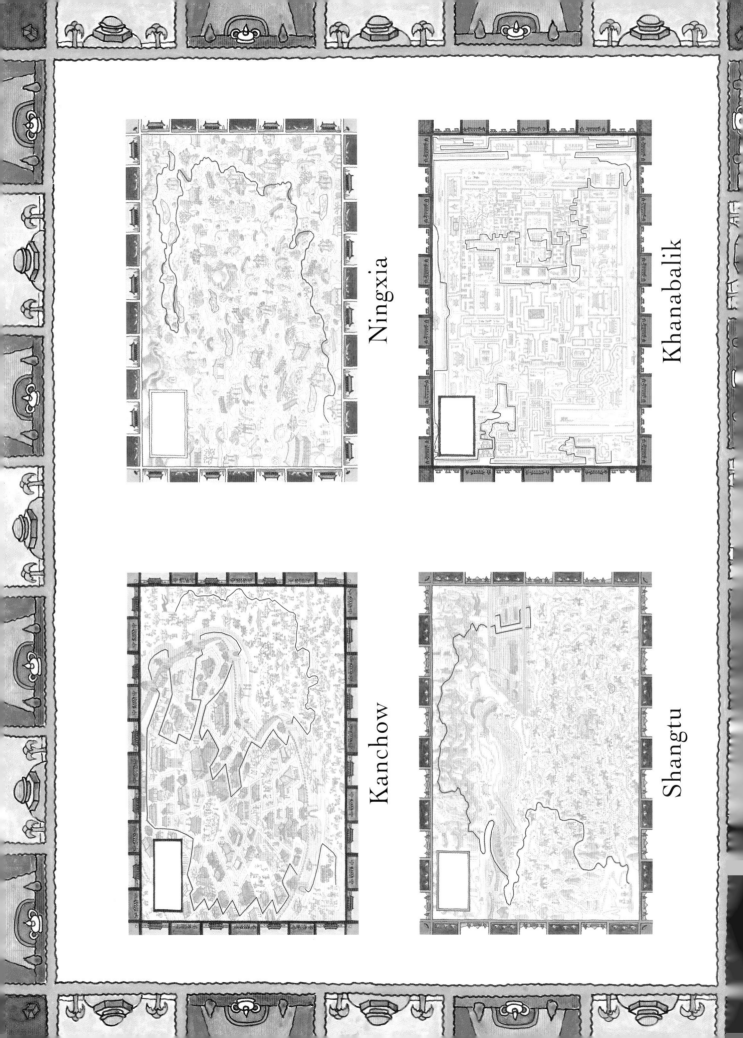

Ningxia

Khanabalik

Kanchow

Shangtu